Lerner SPORTS

SUPER SP

TEAM

INSIDE THE
BOSTON
RED SOX

JON M. FISHMAN

Lerner Publications ◆ Minneapolis

SPORTS THRILLS
MEET
RESEARCH SKILLS

Lerner SPORTS

Free Database Trial: **lernersports.com**

Lerner Publications Company
An imprint of Lerner Publishing Group, Inc.
241 First Avenue North
Minneapolis, MN 55401 USA

For reading levels and more information, look up this title at www.lernerbooks.com.

Main body text set in Aptifer Slab LT Pro / Typeface provided by Linotype AG.

Editor: Brianna Kaiser **Designer:** Kimberly Morales **Photo Editor:** Brianna Kaiser

Library of Congress Cataloging-in-Publication Data

Names: Fishman, Jon M., author.
Title: Inside the Boston Red Sox / Jon M. Fishman.
Description: Minneapolis, MN: Lerner Publications, [2022] | Series: Super sports teams (Lerner sports) | Includes bibliographical references and index. | Audience: Ages 7–11 | Audience: Grades 2–3 | Summary: "Follow the Boston Red Sox from its origins to the present. Sports fans will love learning about the history of one of baseball's most iconic teams, along with its championship wins, greatest players, and more"—Provided by publisher.
Identifiers: LCCN 2021010381 (print) | LCCN 2021010382 (ebook) | ISBN 9781728441726 (library binding) | ISBN 9781728445175 (ebook)
Subjects: LCSH: Boston Red Sox (Baseball team)—Juvenile literature. | World Series (Baseball)—Juvenile literature. | Baseball—United States—Juvenile literature. | Baseball players—United States—Juvenile literature.
Classification: LCC GV875.B62 F57 2022 (print) | LCC GV875.B62 (ebook) | DDC 796.357/640974461—dc23

LC record available at https://lccn.loc.gov/2021010381
LC ebook record available at https://lccn.loc.gov/2021010382

Manufactured in the United States of America
1-49927-49770-8/4/2021

TABLE OF CONTENTS

On October 23, 2018, Mookie Betts hits a single in Game 1 of the World Series.

WORLD SERIES WINNERS

FACTS AT A GLANCE

- In 1903, **BOSTON** won Major League Baseball's (MLB) first World Series.

- The team has played at **FENWAY PARK** since 1912.

- Boston once went 86 seasons between **WORLD SERIES** wins.

- **DAVID ORTIZ** hit 483 home runs with the Red Sox.

The 2018 Boston Red Sox were packed with talented players. Right fielder Mookie Betts won the American League (AL) Most Valuable Player (MVP) award. He led the team to the best record in MLB that year. But in the World Series against the Los Angeles Dodgers, an unexpected hero arose for Boston.

Steve Pearce started the 2018 season with the Toronto Blue Jays. On June 28, Toronto traded the 35-year-old to Boston. The Red Sox were Pearce's seventh MLB team. He was a good player, but he wasn't one of the league's best.

Pearce started at first base in the first two games of the World Series. He went 0–4 as a batter and didn't start Game 3. With Boston leading the series 2–1, Pearce came alive in Game 4. He hit a three-run double and a home run to rack up four RBIs. Boston won 9–6.

Pearce began Game 5 with a bang. He batted in the first inning and smashed a two-run home run. Then he blasted another home run in the eighth inning. Boston beat the Dodgers to win the game and the series. Pearce became the World Series MVP.

The 2018 World Series victory marked Boston's fourth title since 2004. But for almost 90 years, many fans wondered if the team would ever win the World Series again.

Pearce runs the bases after hitting his second home run in Game 5 of the 2018 World Series.

Red Sox players celebrate winning the World Series on October 28, 2018.

Keith Foulke pitches in Game 1 of the 2004 World Series.

FROM AMERICANS TO RED SOX

In the late 19th century, the National League (NL) was the top pro baseball league in North America. But another league was growing. The AL formed in 1901 and began competing with the NL. The AL started with eight teams, including one in Boston.

Boston finished second in the AL in 1901 and third in 1902. In 1903, the AL and NL came together to form MLB. That year, the two league winners met in the first World Series. Boston beat the Pittsburgh Pirates to become MLB's first champions.

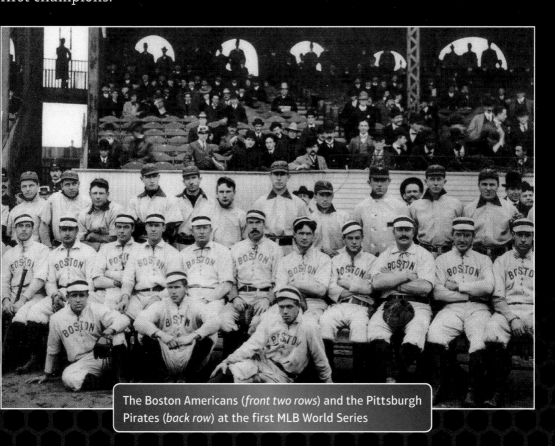

The Boston Americans (*front two rows*) and the Pittsburgh Pirates (*back row*) at the first MLB World Series

The Boston team had many nicknames. Fans called them the Somersets, the Pilgrims, and the Plymouth Rocks. But they were most widely known as the Boston Americans.

After the 1907 season, Americans owner John I. Taylor ordered new uniforms for his team. On the road, Boston wore gray jerseys and pants with blue socks. At home, they had white uniforms with bright red socks. Taylor decided to name the team the Red Sox.

Boston won the World Series as the Red Sox for the first time in 1912. They won it again in 1915, 1916, and 1918. A big reason for Boston's success was pitcher Babe Ruth.

Babe Ruth in 1916

Ruth pitched for the Red Sox from 1914 to 1919.

Ruth pitched 14 innings in Game 2 of the 1916 World Series and allowed just one run. In Game 1 of the 1918 World Series, he pitched nine innings without giving up a run. He pitched 17 World Series innings that year and allowed only two runs. But in 1919, he proved that he was a better batter than a pitcher. He bashed 29 home runs that season. No one else in the AL hit more than 10.

At the time, Ruth was the most exciting player in baseball. He asked the Red Sox for more money. But Harry Frazee, who had become the team owner in 1916, didn't want to pay more. Ruth had a lot of talent, but he caused problems too. He often stayed out too late at night, and he wanted to stop pitching.

The New York Yankees wanted to trade for Ruth. But they didn't have any players the Red Sox wanted. Instead, Frazee sold Ruth's contract to the Yankees after the 1919 season for $100,000.

With the Yankees, Ruth became the greatest player in baseball history, earning nicknames such as the Great Bambino. He hit 54 home runs in 1920, and he was just getting started. He finished his career with 714 big flies, a record that stood for almost 40 years. He also helped New York win the World Series four times.

Ruth slides home for the Yankees during a game in 1925.

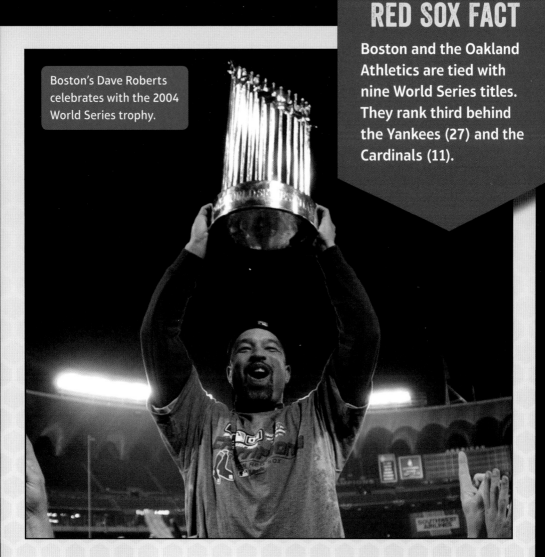

Boston's Dave Roberts celebrates with the 2004 World Series trophy.

As the Yankees won, the Red Sox faded. Boston finished 1920 in fifth place in the AL. They didn't make it back to the World Series until 1946, losing to the St. Louis Cardinals. The Red Sox lost the World Series in 1967, 1975, and 1986. Fans joked that the team had been cursed by selling Babe Ruth to New York. They called it the Curse of the Bambino.

Boston finally broke their World Series losing streak in 2004. They beat the Cardinals in four games to win the title. The Red Sox were ready to begin a new era of winning.

On October 17, 2004, David Ortiz hits a home run in Game 4 of the American League Championship Series (ALCS).

AMAZING MOMENTS

Red Sox history is full of incredible games and plays. On April 20, 1912, the Red Sox played the first regular season game at their new home, Fenway Park. They beat the New York Highlanders 7–6 in extra innings. In 1913, the Highlanders changed their name to the Yankees.

Fenway was home to four World Series–winning Red Sox teams between 1912 and 1918. Then Boston played 27 seasons without reaching MLB's championship series again. But in midsummer of 1946, they were the top team in the AL and had the best record in MLB.

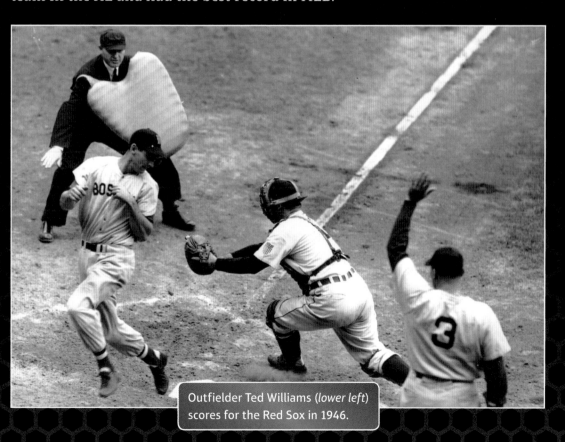

Outfielder Ted Williams (*lower left*) scores for the Red Sox in 1946.

Left to right: Dom DiMaggio, Mickey Vernon, and Ted Williams were among the top 10 hitters in the AL in 1946.

On July 9, the regular season paused for the All-Star Game. The AL all-stars took on the NL all-stars at Fenway. Boston players Dom DiMaggio, Johnny Pesky, and Ted Williams were the first three hitters for the AL.

DiMaggio hit a single, and Pesky went hitless. But Williams carried his team to victory. He had four hits, including two home runs. His five RBIs are tied for the most in All-Star Game history. The AL crushed the NL 12–0. Williams couldn't carry his team in the World Series, though. The Red Sox lost to the Cardinals in seven games.

Boston played 20 seasons without reaching the World Series again. They finally made it back in 1967, losing once more to the Cardinals in seven games. In 1975, the Red Sox lost the World Series to the Cincinnati Reds. Then the New York Mets beat Boston in 1986.

In 2004, the Red Sox had one of the best regular-season records in MLB. They faced the Yankees, their longtime rivals, in the ALCS. The Yankees won the first three games, including a huge 19–8 win in Game 3.

It looked like Boston's season was finished. No team had ever won an MLB playoff series after losing the first three games. But the Red Sox didn't give up.

The Red Sox and the Yankees went into extra innings in Game 4. With a runner on base in the 12th inning, and the teams tied 4–4,

David Ortiz took a massive swing for Boston. He launched the ball over the right-field fence for a game-winning home run. The Fenway crowd roared as Ortiz ran around the bases.

The next game also went to extra innings, and Ortiz came through again. He smacked an RBI single in the 14th to give Boston the win. In Game 6, the Red Sox scored four in the fourth inning to win by two runs. Then they crushed the Yankees 10–3 in Game 7 to win the ALCS.

Topping the Yankees was an amazing feat. But Boston wasn't finished. In the World Series, the Red Sox swept the Cardinals in four games to win their first MLB championship in 86 years. The Curse of the Bambino was broken.

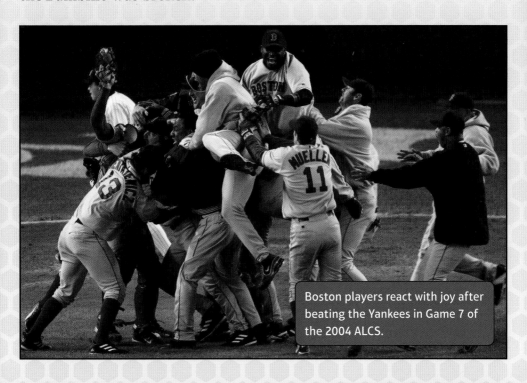

Boston players react with joy after beating the Yankees in Game 7 of the 2004 ALCS.

Ted Williams hit 521 career home runs in his 19 seasons with the Red Sox.

RED SOX SUPERSTARS

The Red Sox have a history of more than 120 MLB seasons. Throughout the years, the team has had far too many great players to cover all of them. One of the first was Cy Young. He pitched for Boston from 1901 to 1908. During that time, he won a shocking 192 games. From 1956 to 1966, the Cy Young Award was given to the best pitcher in MLB. Since 1967, MLB has given the award each season to the best pitcher in the AL and the best pitcher in the NL.

Cy Young in 1905

Ted Williams began his Red Sox career in 1939 and was an immediate hitting sensation. He had a .327 batting average his first year and followed it up with a .344 average. In 1941, he batted .406. No batter has hit .400 or more for a season since then.

Williams had power to go along with his high batting averages. His 521 career home runs are tied for 20th on the all-time list. He reached

Williams crosses home plate after hitting a home run.

On July 23, Carl Yastrzemski makes a catch to stop a home run in the 1969 All-Star Game.

that total despite missing three full seasons serving in the US military during World War II (1939–1945) and missing most of the 1952 and 1953 seasons serving in the Korean War (1950–1953).

Carl Yastrzemski played first base and left field for the Red Sox for 23 seasons. In 1967, he won the Triple Crown by leading the AL in batting average (.326), home runs (44), and RBIs (121). No AL player won the Triple Crown again until Miguel Cabrera in 2012.

Roger Clemens pitches in Game 2 of the 1986 World Series.

Roger Clemens might have been the best pitcher in Red Sox history. While pitching for Boston from 1984 to 1996, Clemens won the 1986 MVP award and three Cy Young Awards. Ortiz started his career with the Minnesota Twins, hitting 58 home runs in six seasons. Then, in 14 seasons with Boston, he blasted 483 homers. The list of great Red Sox players goes on and on.

J. D. Martinez slides home to score a run. Martinez joined the Red Sox in 2018 and led the team with 43 home runs that season.

Red Sox players come together on the field to celebrate winning the 2013 World Series.

AIMING HIGH

After more than 100 seasons, Fenway is the oldest ballpark still in use in MLB. Its most notable feature is the Green Monster. The 37-foot-high (11 m) wall in left field is unlike any other outfield wall in the league. Batters must hit the ball high and far to clear the wall for a home run.

The Red Sox built the wall in 1934 and covered it with advertisements. In 1947, workers cleared the wall. They painted it green, giving the Green Monster its nickname.

Since 2003, Fenway Park's Green Monster has had seats for fans.

When the Red Sox ended their World Series losing streak, they began a winning streak. The team followed up their 2004 breakthrough with World Series wins in 2007, 2013, and 2018. The main reason for their success is the amazing talent of the team's players. But superstars like Xander Bogaerts, Rafael Devers, and J. D. Martinez are expensive. In 2021, Boston paid its players more than $175 million, one of the highest totals in the league.

Boston's long history and success on the field make them one of the most popular MLB teams. The pressure to win is constant in pro baseball, but the Red Sox have shown they can handle it. Fans will get to watch their favorite players do incredible things at Fenway Park for years to come.

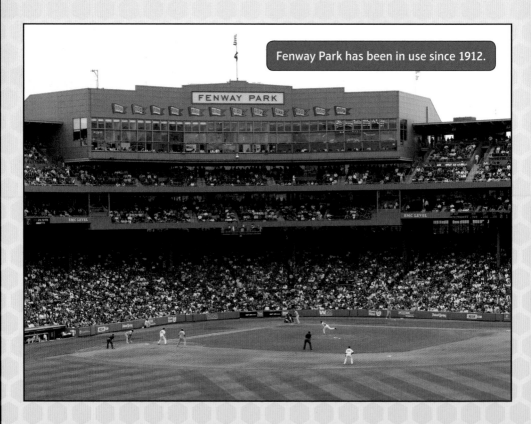

Fenway Park has been in use since 1912.

Rafael Devers blasts a three-run home run against the Yankees in 2021.

Mookie Betts

RED SOX
SEASON RECORD
HOLDERS

HITS

1. Wade Boggs, 240 (1985)
2. Tris Speaker, 222 (1912)
3. Mookie Betts, 214 (2016)
   Wade Boggs, 214 (1988)
5. Adrian Gonzalez, 213 (2011)
   Dustin Pedroia, 213 (2008)
   Jim Rice, 213 (1978)

HOME RUNS

1. David Ortiz, 54 (2006)
2. Jimmie Foxx, 50 (1938)
3. David Ortiz, 47 (2005)
4. Jim Rice, 46 (1978)
5. Manny Ramirez, 45 (2005)

STOLEN BASES

1. Jacoby Ellsbury, 70 (2009)
2. Tommy Harper, 54 (1973)
3. Jacoby Ellsbury, 52 (2013)
   Tris Speaker, 52 (1912)
5. Jacoby Ellsbury, 50 (2008)

WINS

1. Smoky Joe Wood, 34 (1912)
2. Cy Young, 33 (1901)
3. Cy Young, 32 (1902)
4. Cy Young, 28 (1903)
5. Cy Young, 26 (1904)

STRIKEOUTS

1. Pedro Martinez, 313 (1999)
2. Chris Sale, 308 (2017)
3. Roger Clemens, 291 (1988)
4. Pedro Martinez, 284 (2000)
5. Smoky Joe Wood, 258 (1912)

SAVES

1. Tom Gordon, 46 (1998)
2. Craig Kimbrel, 42 (2018)
   Derek Lowe, 42 (2000)
4. Jonathan Papelbon, 41 (2008)
5. Jeff Reardon, 40 (1991)
   Ugueth Urbina, 40 (2002)

GLOSSARY

big fly: a home run

double: a hit in baseball that allows the batter to reach second base

era: an important period of history

extra inning: an inning added to the end of a game if the score is tied

major league: the top level of pro baseball in North America

pro: short for professional, taking part in an activity to make money

RBI: a run in baseball that is driven in by a batter

regular season: when all the teams in a league play against one another to decide the playoff teams

rival: a person or group that tries to defeat or be more successful than another

single: a hit in baseball that allows the batter to reach first base

start: to be in the lineup at the beginning of a game

LEARN MORE

Boston Red Sox
https://www.mlb.com/redsox

Fishman, Jon M. *Baseball's G.O.A.T.: Babe Ruth, Mike Trout, and More*. Minneapolis: Lerner Publications, 2020.

Monson, James. *Behind the Scenes Baseball*. Minneapolis: Lerner Publications, 2020.

Red Sox History
https://www.mlb.com/redsox/history

Sports Illustrated Kids—Baseball
https://www.sikids.com/baseball

Whiting, Jim. *Boston Red Sox*. Mankato, MN: Creative Education, 2021.

INDEX

PHOTO ACKNOWLEDGMENTS

Image credits: AP Photo/Elise Amendola, p. 4; AP Photo/David J. Phillip, p. 6; AP Photo/Jae C. Hong, p. 7; AP Photo/Winslow Townson, p. 8; Wikimedia Commons (CC 2.0), p. 9; Glasshouse Images/Alamy Stock Photo, p. 10; Everett Collection Historical/Alamy Stock Photo, p. 11; AP Photo, pp. 12, 15, 16, 20; AP Photo/Charles Rex Arbogast, p. 13; Reuters/Alamy Stock Photo, pp. 14, 17; Alon Alexander/Alamy Stock Photo, p. 18; Niday Picture Library/Alamy Stock Photo, p. 19; AP Photo/Anonymous, p. 21; AP Photo/Kathy Kmonicek, p. 22; AP Photo/Chris O'Meara, p. 23; AP Photo/Kydpl Kyodo, p. 24; aceshot1/Shutterstock.com, p. 25; Eric Broder Van Dyke/Shutterstock.com, p. 26; AP Photo/Steven Senne, p. 27; AP Photo/Albert Pena, p. 28.

Design element: Master3D/Shutterstock.com.

Cover: Billie Weiss/Boston Red Sox/Getty Images.